Floods and Mudslides

Disaster & Survival

Bonnie J. Ceban

Enslow Publishers, Inc.

40 Industrial Road   PO Box 38
Box 398   Aldershot
Berkeley Heights, NJ 07922 Hants GU12 6BP
USA   UK

http://www.enslow.com

Library of Congress Cataloging-in-Publication Data:

Ceban, Bonnie J.
    Floods and mudslides : disaster & survival / Bonnie J. Ceban.
        p. cm. — (Deadly disasters)
    Includes bibliographical references and index.
    ISBN 0-7660-2389-3
    1. Floods—Juvenile literature. 2. Landslides—Juvenile literature. I. Title.
II. Series.
    GB1399.C43 2005
    363.34'93—dc22

                                   2004028113

Printed in the United States of America

10 9 8 7 6 5 4 3 2 1

To Our Readers: We have done our best to make sure all Internet addresses in
this book were active and appropriate when we went to press. However, the
author and the publisher have no control over and assume no liability for the
material available on those Internet sites or on other Web sites they may link to.
Any comments or suggestions can be sent by e-mail to comments@enslow.com or
to the address on the back cover.

Illustration Credits: Associated Press, AP, pp. 1, 7, 8, 9, 12, 16, 19, 21, 22, 25,
27, 28, 30, 33, 34, 41; Associated Press, THE BERKSHIRE EAGLE, p. 14;
Associated Press, THE POST-CRESCENT, p. 39; Associated Press, STOCKTON
RECORD, p. 15; Associated Press, UN/MINUSTAH, p. 4; Associated Press,
WEST CENTRAL TRIBUNE, p. 38.

Cover Illustration: Associated Press, AP

Contents

The city of Gonaives, Haiti, was completely flooded by Tropical Storm Jeanne.

CHAPTER

1

A Record-Breaking Season

HURRICANE SEASON 2004 BROUGHT TERRIBLE flooding. It was the first time in history that four massive tropical systems hit Florida in one season. That four-blow hit caused billions of dollars in damage. Each storm brought another round of terrible rains. Entire areas were flooded out. Haiti also suffered severe flooding. The flooding caused death, sickness, and injury throughout the small country.

"Help me, I am going to die . . . "

Tropical Storm Jeanne produced major flash floods, or floods that occur very quickly. The flooding killed about nineteen hundred people in Haiti. It left nine hundred people missing and presumed dead. The waters rose quickly. They took people by surprise. Many had nowhere to go.[1]

Héber Pélissier, president of the Gonaives chamber of commerce, watched the waters rise from his home's balcony. "The water took several cars with it, and then the panic started. It began to get dark, and I heard cries: 'Help me, I am going to die, save me, I am drowning.'"

The waters rose past the first story of his home. Bodies floated by. His family stood helpless. Pélissier gathered them to pray. "I had this belief deep inside me that there is a limit to the fury of God," Pélissier said. "I said to God, 'Many have died here. This is it. We don't want any more to die.'"[2] Many did die that day. People were swept away in the rush of water.

There were hardships even after the flooding stopped. Water and food were difficult to find. Houses were covered in mud. They were wet with water. There was no clean place to stay. "There is no [drinking] water, no electricity, no communication," Gonaives mayor Calixte Valentin said. "Many people don't have a place to sleep."[3]

Large groups of people left. They went in search of a safe place for their families. "There is no way to stay here anymore," said Medira

> **"We don't want any more to die."**
>
> —Héber Pélissier, president of the Gonaives, Haiti, chamber of commerce

6

A woman pleads for food and water as she and other flood survivors wait in line at a relief distribution center.

Jarmis. Jarmis, forty-five, decided to flee. He left the area with his family. Their homes were destroyed. "There are so many deaths that this place stinks, and there is nothing to eat and nothing to drink."[4]

Aid workers tried to pass out supplies. People were desperate for food and water. The supplies were often stolen. Maita Alvarez was one of the people handing out clean water. "Some people have been drinking dirty water where dead bodies were floating. It's appalling." The conditions would take months to improve.[5]

Four-Storm Flood

The same storm that created problems in Haiti went on to hit the United States. It and three other storms ripped through Florida within a period of two months. The damage from the storms, much of it due to flooding, left Florida in a state of emergency.

Hurricane Charley came first. It went through Florida in the middle of August 2004. Charley left $20 billion in damage. Thousands of people were instantly homeless. Thirteen people died. People were just starting to pick up the pieces when Hurricane Frances formed.[6]

Frances came through two weeks after Charley. Next was Hurricane Ivan. Finally, Jeanne, upgraded to a hurricane, arrived at the end of September.

Hurricane Jeanne came across Florida with 120-mile-per-hour winds. It hit Florida in almost the same place as Hurricane Frances.[7]

Hundreds of grapefruit float in a flooded grove in Vero Beach, Florida. It is estimated that two-thirds of the grapefruit crop was ruined.

8

Marie Hobock of Vero Beach, Florida, talks about how the flood waters from Hurricane Jeanne damaged her home.

Each of the four major storms brought more rain. The buildup created major flooding. The flooding caused water damage to homes. The winds ripped off roofs, allowing the rain in and causing the water to rise inside the buildings more quickly.

People in Florida were devastated by the disasters. "Every single weekend I think, 'Oh my God, I've got to sit through another one of these,'" said Eden Healt of Tampa. "You get mentally tired and emotionally and physically, just tired. Like a zombie going through your day."[8]

Many people felt the same way. The damage, waters, and loss were too much. "Look at my furniture," said eighty-six-year-old Julie Monti. Her home was completely destroyed. Everything inside had water damage.[9]

Governor Jeb Bush was amazed by the force of the storms. "This is unprecedented; there's been nothing like it," he said. "Certainly it's the largest series of natural disasters we've faced."[10]

> "Oh my God, I've got to sit through another one of these."
>
> —Eden Healt, flood survivor.

The series of disasters left thousands of people homeless. It left dozens dead. The storms and flooding left tragedy everywhere they went.[11]

Studying Floods and Mudslides

A FLOOD OCCURS WHEN WATER SPILLS OUT OF ITS natural boundaries and onto dry land. This overflow happens after a lot of rain. Today, people study the causes of floods so that they can better prepare to battle these disasters.

Too Much Rain

Floods are usually caused by rain. There must be steady rains, in large amounts, for a flood to occur.

A flood is often a long time in the making. Rivers, lakes, ponds, and streams need to get very full after long periods of rain. Also, after a lot of rain, the ground becomes saturated, or "full of water." When the ground is saturated, the rain cannot sink in. Water will begin to lie on top of the land.

As the rain continues, the water will overflow the rivers, lakes, ponds, or streams. It cannot sink into the saturated ground. The land near a body of water—called the floodplain—will then flood, often causing damage to homes and other buildings.

Hurricanes, monsoons, and typhoons can drop huge amounts of water very quickly. This can cause floods to happen in a matter of hours or even minutes.[1]

Flash Floods

A flash flood occurs with little to no warning. Flash floods do not have to happen next to a river. They can happen

A flash flood in Boscastle, Cornwall, in northwestern England, carried these cars down the valley and buried them in mud.

anywhere there is a buildup of water. In cities, water can overflow from storm drains. Flash floods also often occur in mountainous areas. Rainwater runs down mountain slopes and floods canyons. Flash floods can cause water levels to rise within minutes to as much as thirty feet.[2] This is very dangerous because people in the area are often caught off guard.

Floodplains

The land next to a river is called a floodplain. A floodplain is very low-lying land. When a river overflows with water, it spills into the floodplain. Most rivers naturally spill into their floodplains every few years. This only becomes a problem for people who live in the floodplain region.

A town or city in a floodplain is always in danger of flooding. Because of the danger, people must try to protect themselves. Systems have been created to keep water in the rivers.

Levees, Dikes, and Sandbags

One major way the people try to protect land is through levees. A levee is a bank built along a river to protect land from flooding. It is usually covered with concrete. This creates a very tall wall designed to keep water in place. When the river starts to flood, levees keep huge amounts of water from leaving the river. It takes a massive amount of water to break through a levee system.

Another type of wall is called a dike. This wall is built closer to the river water than a levee. A levee is built to keep very high water in place. A dike is built to contain smaller amounts of water. Both walls are used together to create the best possible protection against floods.

People use sandbags to line streets, driveways, and neighborhoods. Sandbags are also placed around buildings. These keep a small amount of street flooding out of homes and businesses. Sometimes, people of a town work together

The land around the Housatonic River in Lenox, Massachusetts, makes up that body of water's floodplain. It is this area that will flood if heavy rains saturate the area.

The Bacon Island Road levee broke during a 2004 storm. About a three-hundred-foot section of the levee was swept away, allowing floodwater to pour through.

to sandbag unprotected areas of a river bank. However, if the flooding is too high, the sandbags cannot help.

Mudslides

Mudslides can occur during a flood. A mudslide happens along a sloped area of land. Once the land is saturated with water, it can begin to move. It will often slide slowly at first. But, it quickly picks up speed. Then, more mud and debris start to slide. Soon, there is a very large and

This mudslide in La Conchita, California, killed ten people on January 10, 2005.

dangerous amount of land sliding quickly down a slope. If houses or businesses are built on land prone to slides or land beneath a slide, they can end up entirely covered by mud. A mudslide can get so big that it can cover a thirty-foot building.[3]

Floods and mudslides occur around the world. People of many countries have survived these hardships and go on to tell their amazing stories.

Mudslide in Venezuela

ON DECEMBER 16, 1999, OVER SIXTY MILES OF LAND were covered in a mudslide in Venezuela. Residents' lives would never be the same.

Dash for the Third Floor

The floods surprised many people. Doris Segui gathered with over twenty others in a ground-floor apartment. They thought that it was safe. Then someone yelled, "Not here. Let's get out!" Doris explains, "We turned around and saw a wave of mud coming towards us. We ran to the third floor. But the woman, her husband and children, decided to take another route. The river [of mud]

"We turned around and saw a wave of mud coming toward us."

—Doris Segui, flood survivor.

Los Corales, Venezuela, was devastated by the 1999 flood.

swept them away." Doris watched helplessly while people disappeared beneath the mud. Teenagers swimming in a nearby pool were caught up in the waves of mud. "It all happened in 30 seconds. We were very lucky. We'll go back to start again," Doris said.[1]

Mudslides are very unpredictable. Even though certain areas are at risk of mudslides, no one knows exactly when a mudslide will happen. Venezuela residents did not expect such horrible slides.

19

Rising Waters in the Basement

Luis Landaeta, his wife, and their two children were trapped in their basement. Bodies of those who died were also there. Luis found a cell phone on one of the victims. He then called a local radio station for help. "I don't know what to do. My chest hurts. I'm desperate. It's all just mud. My son is sleeping on mud," Luis cried. He was hysterical with fear. "Please get us out of here. It's very dark." Luis was too upset to talk. He handed the phone to his five-year-old son. "Yes, I'm very calm, but my Daddy isn't," his son said.

President Hugo Chavez was able to talk to the Landaeta family on the phone. "Be calm, brother. Be very calm," the president said. "Good evening, Mr. President," Luis replied, "Listen, I am trapped, my children are here, my mother died about an hour ago. Tell the people coming to get us they have to bring tools to break down the walls." Luis continued to talk, but his wife died before rescue workers could come to her rescue.[2]

President Hugo Chavez tried to comfort many people. He was inspired by community support. "The people of Venezuela have a seed of solidarity, which only

> "... my mother died about an hour ago."
>
> —Luis Landaeta, mudslide survivor.

Venezuelan president Hugo Chavez gives paratroopers a pep talk. The paratroopers are about to go on a mission to rescue flood survivors who are stranded on the tops of buildings.

needs something as big as this to wake it up and realize its potential," the president proclaimed.[3]

In the End

In total, the mudslides affected over two hundred fifty thousand people. Over one hundred fifty thousand people lost their homes. Some towns were buried by mud. A small town named Carmen de Uria lost over twenty-nine hundred homes. There were only three thousand homes in the town before the slides.[4]

21

Even worse, many people were lost and died in the mud. Over thirty thousand people are estimated to have died. Foreign Minister Jose Vicente Rangel spoke of the tragedy. "There are bodies in the sea, bodies buried under the mud, bodies everywhere," he said.[5]

In many areas, thousands of bodies remained under twenty feet or more of mud. These areas were considered

A mudslide buried much of the village of Carmen de Uria, Venezuela. As many as two thousand of the townspeople were killed.

"unsearchable." Instead, the bodies were left there. Then, that land was set apart to honor those who had died.[6]

Venezuelans lost a lot that December. Yet, they also learned a lot. Many of the houses were not built to withstand flooding or mudslides. Some of the poor towns on the coast were built without permission. People thought that they were making a better life. However, it was on a very dangerous slope. Archbishop of La Guaira, Francisco de Guruceaga, commented on the event. "In one night everything collapsed like a house of cards," he said. "Nature always reclaims its own, and we cannot repeat the same urban mistakes that brought us this disaster."[7]

American Floods and Mudslides

L IKE MOST OTHER COUNTRIES, THE UNITED STATES has seen its share of floods.

Flooding in the New Year

In January 2005, Southern California saw some of its worst flooding in years. From January 6 to January 10, heavy rains saturated several counties in the area. Over $100 million dollars in damage was caused.[1] About half of this damage was done to the roads and highways.[2] Some roads were completely washed out or blocked with debris.

Ventura County farmers alone had at least $38 million in damage to crops.[3] The flood waters killed some plants. In other cases, the excess water caused fruit to rot. It also caused fungus to grow, which killed the crops. Some

24

A house sinks into the Santa Clara River in California. Luckily, the house had already been evacuated.

California farms had over twelve inches of rain in the five-day period.[4]

The Deadly La Conchita Mudslide

After days of rain, sixty-one-year-old Greg Ray was outside his home in La Conchita, California. Suddenly, he saw a wall of mud coming toward him. Ray dove between two cars. Though this quick thinking saved his life, he was unable to escape injury.

On January 10, 2005, part of La Conchita, California, was buried when a hillside collapsed on the small village. The mudslide, which killed ten people, deeply affected the small community of 260 residents. Ray was pulled from the mud by rescuers and later spoke from his hospital bed: "I lost people that I love, and the only reason that I'm alive . . . I don't know."[5]

The Wallet family was the hardest hit by the mudslide. Jimmy Wallet had left with one of his daughters to get ice cream. When they returned, their house was completely buried. In a daze, Jimmy Wallet tried to help rescuers locate the rest of his family. However, his wife, Mechelle, and three other daughters—Hannah, ten; Raven, six; and Paloma, two—were found dead.

In all, four hundred thousand tons of mud fell on La Conchita that day.[6] Officials feared another collapse. Town members were quickly evacuated. Some of the homes would have to stay buried because moving the earth on them could trigger another slide. Sheriff Bob Brooks highlighted the danger, saying, "The La Conchita community is a geologically hazardous area. We do not recommend that people return to this area or the people who stay here remain here."[7] Even if the workers did not move any earth, the whole town still was in danger of being buried by more mudslides.

Jimmy Wallet (center) whose wife and three children were killed in the La Conchita mudslide.

The Toll on California

Including the ten killed in the mudslide, the Southern California floods killed twenty-eight people. Governor Arnold Schwarzenegger declared a state of emergency in eight counties. A memorial was held for the mudslide victims. Jimmy Wallet was grateful for the outpouring of support: "This community is all heart."[8]

27

The Flood of '93

"There's just so much water. Water, water, everywhere," said Denise Yale. Like many others, Yale felt overwhelmed by the Great Flood of 1993. In total, the Mississippi River flooded areas in nine different states. This huge flood caused $18 billion in damage. Many towns were completely underwater. Homes were washed away. Even then, the water kept rising.[9]

Water from the Mississippi River floods farmland near Columbia, Illinois. The house on the right was forced off its foundation by the floodwater and carried downstream.

"The river won't stop coming," said Paul Arnold, the flood coordinator in Grafton, Illinois, "and people are really getting frustrated and depressed. I've seen a lot of eyes filled with tears."[10]

Grafton was not the only town shocked by the floodwaters. In Des Moines, Iowa, the floods ruined drinking water for two hundred fifty thousand people. It also cut off electricity to thousands of homes. Restored electric power came in a week, while drinking water took nearly a month. Emergency trucks brought in some water for distribution. However, rationing water became necessary. "The water is for drinking only," the mayor said. "It's not for bathing or anything else. We are in pretty good shape. It's not a panic situation."[11]

Battling for the Levees

Farther down the Mississippi River, floodwaters threatened St. Louis, Missouri. "We have quite a fight on our hands," said Lloyd Dolbeare, an emergency service coordinator. Sandbagging and securing the levees began immediately. Levees began to break in and around the city. However, the efforts continued. "They're tired, they're beat. They're falling down with their shovels in their hands," said John Carrier of those working on the levees. The work continued, though, because every little bit would keep the city that much drier.[12]

Resident volunteers take a break from building a sandbag dike in Windsor Heights, Iowa. The people of the town were trying to stop the floodwaters from the rising local rivers.

Unsafe Feelings

As flooding continued across the Midwestern states, many people had a big decision to make. Would they stay, or would they leave? "A lot of people who weren't here before are really upset about the flooding," said Julie Zimerman. "I don't like it either. I bought my house in

30

1986 and had to move out six weeks later because of flooding. But I was baptized here, my family's here, so I'll clean up and start all over. Most of the time the Mississippi is like an old friend."[13]

Many others had a different take on things. "This has become too much, how long can we take this? I want to live a normal life. I want my children to play in our back-yard again," said flood survivor Amy Despoint. "We're going to move on. The Mississippi is beautiful. But, it's not worth this price."[14]

A Historic American Flood

Although some flooding is a part of life on a river, the "Great Flood" of 1993 was one of the worst in United States history. It occurred because of nearly a year of large rainfalls, followed by heavy snowmelt. In total, fifty-two people drowned because of the floods. Hundreds more were injured.[15]

"It's going to take a long time for the water to go down," said the spokeswoman for the Army Corps of Engineers.[16] In many areas, it took months to get the water down. Floods are one of the longest lasting and dirt-iest natural disasters. In particular, this flood was the worst the United States had seen in a century. The cleanup process lasted into 1994, and many smaller towns never fully recovered from all the damage.[17]

Floods in Bangladesh

RESIDENTS OF BANGLADESH WERE IN TROUBLE. THAT trouble was water—more water than they could handle. They were literally up to their necks, or higher, in floodwaters. Worse yet, in July 2004, over 60 percent of the country was covered in that water.

A Severe Monsoon Season

Mohammad Shaheen lives in a single-story brick home in a city called Dhaka. Houses in Dhaka must be built on pillars because floods happen so often. These floods happen because of seasonal monsoons. This means that each year at the same time, there are large amounts of rain and storms.

> "I had to raise the bed with up to six bricks today . . ."
>
> —Mohammed Shaheen, flood survivor.

Some seasons are worse than others. All seasons bring some amount of flooding. These waters were worse than Mohammad had ever seen. "I had to raise the bed with up to six bricks today, but I could not put bricks under the wardrobe as it was too heavy to move," he explained. Water crept into Mohammad's home every day. Each day it arrived a bit higher.[1]

In Dhaka alone, over two hundred sixty thousand people took refuge in shelters. Homes were ruined by water.

Bangladeshi rickshaw pullers try to move down a flooded street. Seasonal monsoon rains were the cause of the widespread flooding.

33

A survivor in Bangladesh sleeps in her flooded house. Other victims sought refuge in shelters.

Many were completely covered in the rising tides. Some residents, desperate to get home, built bamboo bridges to their front doors.[2]

Spreading Diseases

Massive floods do more than just destroy property. They carry diseases and infect water supplies. Over one hundred thousand people in Bangladesh were infected with waterborne diseases. The diseases included dysentery and typhoid. Over sixty people died of diseases. Over four hundred died in the floods.[3]

Diseases spread quicker due to a lack of water-purification tablets. The tablets, which keep drinking water free of disease, were in short supply. "So far, authorities have been able to supply only 2.5 million tablets. At least 90 million are needed," said a public health official. "The situation will get worse when flood survivors return home. They will have to live on whatever they can find to eat. And, muddy water to drink."[4]

34

Struggling in Shelters

Shelters quickly ran out of food. New supplies could not be sent in because of the high waters.

"We have been here for six days," said Aleya Begum. She stayed at the Dhaka shelter. Her nine-month-old baby stayed with her. "Nobody has come with baby food or medicines," she said. Many babies were getting sick from eating adult food.[5]

Many people experienced the same problems. There were not enough supplies to go around. When there were supplies, the water prevented rescue workers from getting it to the people.[6]

> "Nobody has come with baby food or medicines."
>
> —Aleya Begum, flood survivor.

Some of the hardship in Bangladesh may have been avoided if people were better prepared. Being prepared is the key to survival in flood-prone areas.

6

Staying Safe

FLOOD SAFETY IS TIED TO FLOOD AWARENESS. IT IS important to know if you live in a flood-prone area, or floodplain. Families that live in these areas must be prepared. Even families who do not live in a flood-prone area should still be aware of flood safety. Strong storms can cause flooding in any area, even if there are no bodies of water nearby.

Flood Plans

One of the most important parts of flood planning is knowing your risk level. If you do not know if you are in a flood-risk area, it is important to find out. Local emergency management offices can let you know if you are in a flood zone. The National Weather Service is also a good source for current flood zones. Once you know your risk, be alert. A lot of rain can become a problem for a flood-prone area. If areas near your neighborhood have flooded out, yours may be next.

Families should have a disaster plan. Copies of insurance policies, documents, and other valuables should be stored in a waterproof box. Store the box as high as possible, such as on a top shelf or second floor. If possible, store a second copy of all important papers at a location besides your home.

Before the risk of a flood arrives, every family should have a disaster supplies kit available. Gather items that will be necessary in a flood.
• First aid kit and prescription medicines
• Canned food and can opener
• At least 3 gallons (11 liters) of clean drinking water per person
• Protective clothing, rainwear, and bedding
• Battery-powered radio, flashlight, and extra batteries
• Special items for infants, elderly, or disabled family members
• A list of places you can go if ordered to evacuate. Choose more than one place.
• Some spending money in case ATMs and banks are not available
All items should be stored together in a safe place. Kits should be checked at the beginning of each year, and after each use. Any missing items should be restocked.

It is important to include raingear in a flood disaster preparedness kit. This public worker wears raingear as he fights a flood in Willmar, Minnesota.

A family plan should include job assignments. Jobs during a flood emergency can include gathering supplies, tracking weather reports, or preparing the house. If work is shared, a family can act quickly during a flood. Also, keep track of each person's location. Speed and communication are important in an emergency.

Protect Your House

There are a number of other ways to have a flood-ready house. First, make sure that all water heaters are above ground level. It is very important to keep outside water away from the heaters. Also, all electrical panels and connections should be kept as high as possible. Water can create severe damage to the systems. In addition, always keep furniture raised in flood-prone parts of the house. This will protect the furniture should water start to creep in. Keep valuables away from risky areas.

A man in Omro, Wisconsin, tries to protect his house from the rising Fox River. He built a sandbag wall and installed a sump pump. The sump pump takes water from around his house and pumps it back into the river through a hose.

Watches and Warnings

During a flood watch, conditions are possible for a flood to occur. When a flood watch is issued, make sure to pay attention and continue to listen to weather alerts. A flood watch is a good opportunity to get ready. Help your parents move furniture and valuables to higher areas in your home. Gather family members to review your flood disaster plan. Make sure there is gas in the car in case an evacuation is ordered.

A flood warning is issued when a flood is about to occur. If a flood warning is issued, listen carefully to your local radio or television stations for directions. Always follow official orders. Evacuations are used to save lives. If an evacuation is ordered, it is important to leave.

Be ready to leave if a flash flood watch is issued. Flash floods happen quickly, so it is very important to listen to all alerts and instructions. Have a planned escape route ahead of time. The route should move toward higher ground. Get supplies ready and prepare low-lying areas of your home.

If a flash flood warning is issued, evacuate immediately. Follow all instructions from safety workers. Use your planned evacuation route to get to higher ground. Stay away from rivers, streams, creeks, and storm drains. If a road is blocked off, it is for your safety. Do not drive around barricades. If the driver cannot see the road through the water, do not drive through the flooded road. If the car stalls in rising water, abandon it. Immediately climb out of your car and get to higher ground. Come back for your car after the waters have receded. Always look for the safest place for yourself; worry about your car and home after the water is gone.

Floods and mudslides are risky events with many

A family should have more than one escape route. Sometimes, an escape route can be blocked with water or debris. Topanga Canyon Road in California was blocked by a twenty-five-foot high boulder in 2005.

potential dangers. Early preparation, planning, and action are important to ensure the safety of all residents. The National Weather Service, as well as local emergency relief centers, can supply more information on flooding in your area.

If you stay aware and prepare for the worst, you can turn a flood from a family disaster into a story of survival.

41

World's Deadliest Floods

Rank	Date	Place	Description	Deaths
1	July–August 1931	China	Yangtze River floods, drowning people and causing disease and starvation.	3.7 million
2	1228	Friesland, Holland	Sea floods.	100,000
3	August 1971	Hanoi, North Vietnam	Red River Delta is flooded by heavy rains.	100,000
4	August 5, 1975	Yangtze River, China	Sixty-three dams were damaged or collapsed, causing flooding and starvation from damaged crops.	80,000–200,000
5	August 1954	Tehran, Iran	Heavy rains cause flooding.	10,000
6	December 15–16, 1999	Northern Venezuela	Heavy rains cause flooding and mudslides.	5,000–20,000
7	Summer 1998	Central and Northeast China	Yangtze River floods.	3,000
8	May 31, 1889	Johnstown, Pennsylvania	South Fork Dam gives way.	2,200
9 (tie)	October 9, 1963	Italy	A landslide slams into the Vaiont Dam, causing flooding.	2,000
9 (tie)	May 18–26, 2004	Dominican Republic and Haiti	Soleil River floods from heavy rains, causing mudslides	2,000

Note: Floods caused by tsunamis were not listed for the purposes of this chart.

Chapter Notes

Chapter 1: A Record-Breaking Season

1. Deborah Sontag and Lydia Polgreen, "Storm-Battered Haiti's Endless Crises Deepen," *The New York Times*, October 16, 2004, p. A1.

2. Ibid.

3. James C. McKinley Jr., "Weary, Angry Haitians Dig Out of Storm," *The New York Times*, September 24, 2004, p. A3.

4. Ibid.

5. Ibid.

6. Abby Goodnough, "Hurricane Charley: The Overview; Florida Digs Out As Mighty Storm Rips Northward," *The New York Times*, August 15, 2004, p. 1-1.

7. Abby Goodnough, "Another Hurricane Roars Across Mid-Florida," *The New York Times*, September 27, 2004, p. A22.

8. Ibid.

9. Ibid.

10. Ibid.

11. Ibid.

Chapter 2: Studying Floods and Mudslides

1. Jack Williams, *The Weather Book* (New York: Vintage Books, 1997), pp. 94–97.

2. "Flash Floods: The Deadly Force of Nature," *BBC News*, May 18, 2001, <http://news.bbc.co.uk/1/hi/sci/tech/1337404.stm> (April 19, 2005).

3. Reader's Digest, *Weather* (New York: Reader's Digest Association Inc., 1997), pp. 104–109.

Chapter 3: Mudslide in Venezuela

1. "Desperate tales from the disaster zone," *BBC News*, December 21, 1999, <http://news.bbc.co.uk/1/hi/world/monitoring/media_reports/573705.stm> (November 23, 2004).

2. Ibid.

3. "Venezuelans 'more united than ever,'" *BBC News*,

December 22, 1999, <http://news.bbc.co.uk/1/hi/world/monitoring/media_reports/575165.stm> (November 23, 2004).

4. "World rallies to Venezuela's aid," *BBC News*, December 22, 1999, <http://news.bbc.co.uk/1/hi/world/americas/574959.stm> (November 23, 2004).

5. "30,000 feared dead in floods," *BBC News*, December 21, 1999, <http://news.bbc.co.uk/1/hi/world/americas/574077.stm> (November 23, 2004).

6. "Flood survivors brave the hardships," *BBC News*, December 26, 1999, <http://news.bbc.co.uk/1/hi/world/americas/578527.stm> (April 19, 2005).

7. "Desperate tales from the disaster zone," *BBC News*, December 21, 1999, <http://news.bbc.co.uk/1/hi/world/monitoring/media_reports/573705.stm> (April 19, 2005).

Chapter 4: American Floods and Mudslides

1. Alex Viega, "Calif. Storms Said Likely to Cost $100M," *Boston.com*, January 14, 2005, <http://www.boston.com/business/articles/2005/01/14/calif_storms_said_likely_to_cost_100m/> (February 2, 2005).

2. Ibid.

3. Daisy Nguyen, "California Storm Damaged Crops," *Boston.com*, January 19, 2005, <http://www.boston.com/business/articles/2005/01/19/california_storm_damaged_crops/> (February 2, 2005).

4. Ibid.

5. Robert Jablon, "Search Ends for Calif. Mudslide Survivors," *ABC News*, January 14, 2005, <http://abcnews.go.com/US/print?id=411130> (February 2, 2005).

6. Ibid.

7. Ibid.

8. Jeff Wilson, "Memorial Held for Calif. Mudslide Victims," *Boston.com*, January 22, 2005, <http://www.

boston.com/news/nation/articles/2005/01/22/memorial_ held_for_calif_mudslide_victims/> (February 2, 2005).

9. Don Terry, "As Mississippi Swells, Havoc in the Heartland," *The New York Times*, June 30, 1993, p. A12.

10. Don Terry, "Flood Leaves 250,000 Without Water to Drink," *The New York Times*, July 12, 1993 p. A1.

11. Dirk Johnson, "Flooded by Endless Rainfall, Midwest Braces for Still More," *The New York Times*, July 9, 1993, p. 1.

12. Ibid.

13. Don Terry, "In Weary Town, Mississippi Shows Its Might," *The New York Times*, July 3, 1993, p. 1

14. Ibid.

15. Diane Raines Ward, *Water Wars* (New York: Riverhead Books, 2002), p. 161.

16. Terry, "As Mississippi Swells, Havoc in the Heartland."

17. Ward.

Chapter 5: Floods in Bangladesh

1. Parveen Ahmed, "Bangladesh capital inundated as millions suffer in flooded South Asia," *Forest Conservation Portal*, July 29, 2004, <http://forests.org/articles/reader. asp?linkid=33914> (November 23, 2004).

2. Ibid.

3. Julhas Alam, "Death Toll From S. Asia Floods Tops 1,550," *Lexington Herald-Leader*, August 1, 2004, <http://www.dfw. com/mld/kentucky/9297979.htm?1c> (November 23, 2004).

4. Anis Ahmed, "Disease and hunger spread as South Asia floods ease," Yahoo! *India News*, August 2, 2004, <http://in. news.yahoo.com/040802/137/2fail.html> (November 23, 2004).

5. Alam.

6. Ibid.

Chapter 6: Staying Safe

1. "Flood and Flash Flood," *American Red Cross*, n.d., <http://www.redcross.org/services/disaster/0,1082,0_585_,00. html> (November 30, 2004).

Glossary

dike—A wall built close to a river in order to collect small amounts of floodwaters.

flash flood—A fast-paced flood where waters can rise over a foot in one hour; comes with very little warning, usually accompanied by large rainfalls.

flood—An overflow of water out of its natural boundaries and onto land, homes, and properties.

levee—A bank built along a river to protect land from flooding.

mudslide—The movement of mud, rock, and debris down a sloped land area due to saturated land and/or floodwaters.

National Weather Service—An agency that provides weather forecasts and warnings, as well as a database of climate statistics, to the United States.

sandbags—Bags of sand used to block and redirect the floodwaters.

Further Reading

Books

Allan, Tony. *Wild Water: Floods.* Chicago: Raintree, 2005.

Eagen, Rachel. *Flood and Monsoon Alert!* New York: Crabtree Publication Co., 2005.

Moore, Richard and Jay Barnes. *Faces From the Flood: Hurricane Floyd Remembered.* Chapel Hill: University of North Carolina Press, 2004.

Spilsbury, Louise and Richard. *Raging Floods.* Chicago: Heinemann Library, 2003.

Internet Addresses

FEMA: Floodsmart.gov Flood Planning
<http://www.floodsmart.gov>

National Oceanic and Atmospheric Administration (NOAA): Flood Information
<http://www.noaa.gov>
Scroll down and click on "Weather" under "Science, Service, and Stewardship." Scroll down and click on "Floods."

National Weather Service: Severe Weather Awareness
<http://www.nws.noaa.gov/om/>
Click "Weather Awareness" at the left. Click on "Floods."

Index